Buying and Selling a House

UNITED KINGDOM
Sweet & Maxwell Ltd
London

AUSTRALIA
LBC Information Services Ltd
Sydney

CANADA and USA
Carswell
Toronto

NEW ZEALAND
Brookers
Wellington

SINGAPORE and MALAYSIA
Sweet & Maxwell
Singapore and Kuala Lumpur

What is the Law?

Buying and Selling a House

JAMES K. CANNY

B.A., LL.B., M.A., A.C.I.Arb.

DUBLIN
THOMSON, ROUND HALL
2002

Published in 2002 by
Round Hall Ltd.
43 Fitzwilliam Place
Dublin 2
Ireland

Typeset by
Devlin Editing, Dublin

Printed by
Techman, Ireland

A CIP catalogue record for this book is available from the British Library

ISBN 1-85800-314-8

ABOUT THE AUTHOR

James K. Canny, B.A., LL.B., M.A., A.C.I.Arb., is a practising solicitor and the author of *The Law of Road Transport and Haulage, The Law of Local Government* and *Construction and Building Law*, all of which are published by Thomson Round Hall.

CONTENTS

PREFACE

Most Irish people will either own or want to own their own house at some time in their lives. General advice on house purchase is plentiful and usually well meaning. However, to avoid incurring higher costs and wasting time, the more professional the advice you receive the better. Practical advice would be to visit the property at different times of the day and week to see if there are any problems in the neighbourhood, such as traffic congestion, noise pollution from local businesses or late-night entertainment venues, or parking problems. Professional advice refers to mortgages, deposits, contracts, fees, surveyors, building agreements, development plans, planning permission, stamp duties, title documents, grants and legislation relevant to both purchases and sellers of property. The more you know, the easier the process will be.

The chapters in this book deal with stamp duty, taking out loans or mortgages, new house grants, completing the purchase of a house, purchasing second-hand houses and examining the title documents of houses. **Chapter 8** is devoted to dealing with some problems which may arise after purchasing a house, and the protection which is available to house owners and **Chapter 9** discusses the procedures involved in selling your house. A glossary is included to provide explanations for some of the legal terms encountered in house purchase/selling.

1 FINANCING YOUR HOUSE

1:1 INTRODUCTION

Most people who purchase property will do so with the benefit of a mortgage or a loan. The underlying principle in law is that the borrower (or mortgagor) sells the property to the financial institution (the mortgagee) and buys it back over a defined period and at an agreed rate of interest. Essentially, each type of mortgage has the same basic idea behind it: the property remains in the possession of the mortgagor subject to the mortgage interest of the financial institution. Some mortgages are based on annuity repayments while others are based on an endowment policy (*see* **para 1:2.3**).

Some properties can be mortgaged more than once. However, this is unusual today, as the first mortgage company comes first in priority and their consent must be obtained prior to re-mortgaging. In any case, the modern practice is to obtain a new or larger mortgage from the same mortgage company or to redeem, or pay off, the first mortgage and obtain a new one.

1:2 CHOOSING A MORTGAGE

1:2.1 Length of mortgage

Before choosing which mortgage company to go with, it is important to realise how much the mortgage is going to cost over the full term. A 30-year mortgage is more expensive than a 25-year mortgage, which is in turn more expensive than a 20-year mortgage. Many people choose a long-term mortgage because the mortgage repayments are slightly lower. However, when multiplied over the full term, the real cost of the mortgage becomes apparent. It is advisable to aim to have your mortgage paid off at a time in your life when you may wish to remortgage the property, for instance, for third-level education fees. At today's interest rates, few investments can give the same return as the interest rate on a mortgage.

Borrowers should also be aware that the house insurance and life insurance offered by the mortgage lending institution might not be cheaper than those offered by other financial institutions. Many people feel that there is less work involved in getting their insurance along with their mortgage from the same institution. However, over the lifetime of the mortgage even a slight difference may be a substantial saving. Again, it is quite often just a matter of looking for the best value.

1:2.2 Types of interest rates and mortgages

Borrowers should be aware that there is a difference between the interest rate quoted and the true rate charged over the year, the annual percentage rate (APR). The Consumer Credit Act 1995 obliges all financial institutions to disclose:

1. A full statement of the APR;
2. The cost of the credit at the end of the mortgage period;
3. The monthly repayment; and
4. The likely effect of an increase of 1 per cent in the interest rate.

The APR is the equivalent, on an annual basis, of the present value of all commitments, loans, repayments and charges, future or existing, agreed by the creditor and the consumer. The 1995 Act also introduced a statutory "cooling-off" period to allow consumers 10 days to decide whether or not to proceed with the loan or credit being sought. However, this does not apply to housing loans, as there is often a considerable period of time between signing the letter of loan offer and the draw down of the mortgage (receipt of the loan or mortgage cheque). It is of relevance to most house purchasers, most of whom will have some personal borrowings on top of their mortgage to pay for the initial 10 per cent deposit and/or to furnish their house.

1:2.3 Annuity payments and endowment policies

A dilemma facing many purchasers is the choice of interest rates for house mortgages available to borrowers. There are two different types of mortgages — an annuity and an endowment mortgage.

The annuity mortgage allows the borrower to pay off interest as well as part of the principal borrowed, while the endowment mortgage acts like an investment fund and is designed to pay off the principal when the policy matures. With an endowment policy the money being paid into it is invested with the aim that there should be enough annual growth over the lifetime of the mortgage to repay the entire mortgage. However, there is a grave risk that the policy will not perform well enough to pay off the mortgage at the end of the mortgage period. Anyone with an endowment policy will be given an annual statement showing how their policy is performing. It is important that those policyholders adjust their monthly repayments to ensure that there will be enough to repay the mortgage.

1.2.4 Fixed and variable interest rates

It is important to realise that there is a marked difference between a fixed and variable interest rate. The fixed interest rate can seem good value, but choosing a fixed rate interest mortgage can be a gamble, as interest rates may fall as well as rise. Furthermore, if the property is sold or remortgaged within the time period during which the mortgage rate is fixed, then there will be an early redemption penalty payable, which is a penalty charge by the mortgage company to cover any losses it incurs.

A variable interest rate mortgage is also a gamble, as the rate can go above the initial fixed interest rate. The early redemption penalty is usually not applied to variable interest rate mortgages and the rate can work out to be the best value over the lifetime of the mortgage. However, the variable rate itself may not be the same rate as that received by other borrowers within the same financial institution. In other words, there may be different variable rates applicable to the same mortgages for different people. This is because the starting rate of interest may have been different or there may have been an initial loading of the interest rate. An example of this loading would be where a borrower has obtained a mortgage with the intention of buying either an investment property or a second home. The financial institution may decide that this is a commercial venture and load the interest rate accordingly at the start of the mortgage. When the variable rate is later increased or decreased, the loading remains.

Most people will be aware that when the European Central Bank lowers interest rates, the decrease is not always passed on to mortgage holders or not all of the rate, is passed on. There is always a considerable delay in passing on a decrease — though, funnily, not where there is an increase!

1:3 MORTGAGE TERMS AND CONDITIONS

1:3.1 The letter of loan

The essential point to remember when obtaining a mortgage is that, in law, the letter of loan offer from the financial institution is a mere contract between the financial institution and the borrower. It is always open to the borrower to seek a better contract either from the same or from a different institution. The letter of loan offer is the formal contract document which is issued to the borrower and includes:

- the term of the mortgage;
- the initial interest rate:
- whether it is for one or more years;
- the amount borrowed;
- the APR; and
- the amount which will be paid in total over the full period of the mortgage.

1:3.2 Special conditions

The letter of loan offer may also contain certain special conditions which the borrower will have to fulfil before drawing down the mortgage. One such condition may be the stipulation that the mortgage be drawn down within a defined period, as otherwise a new interest rate will apply or more conditions may be imposed. Several other conditions may be included in the letter of loan offer, some of which may deal with certain legal conditions such as planning permission, title requirements, and so on. Sometimes the mortgage company may insist that a percentage of the mortgage is held back until the construction of the house is completed, or may provide that other existing loans are paid off from the proceeds of the mortgage.

1:3.3 Terms and conditions

The terms and conditions of mortgages vary from one financial institution to another, but the basic terms are the same: the mortgage must be repaid by the agreed monthly repayment at the agreed interest rate. If the mortgage repayments are not made, then penalties are applied to the loan, with the result that interest is applied on the penalty. Legal expenses may also be added to the mortgage, and, again, interest becomes chargeable on these expenses. This means that even though the monthly repayments are eventually made, additional interest is being paid and additional money has been added to the mortgage. If the default occurs early in the mortgage, the net cost can be substantial.

Generally speaking, if the borrower misses two to three instalments, the mortgage has been defaulted and the mortgage company can institute proceedings to take the property from the borrower. The mortgage company can then sell it and either give back any excess money made on the sale or, if the property does not make enough when sold, seek any shortfall from the borrower. It is therefore advisable that borrowers ensure that every monthly repayment is made and check to make sure that the mortgage has been paid. Borrowers need to be aware that it is not up to the mortgage company to inform the borrower that repayments are not being made. The terms of mortgages can vary from one financial institution to the next. However, all mortgages will stipulate that the entire mortgage becomes due if the monthly repayments are not paid after the stated period, or if the mortgagors enter into a composition or arrangement with creditors, which amounts to bankrupty in all but name. This happens if:

- the borrower becomes bankrupt but the High Court has not yet issued made an order declaring his or her bankruptcy;
- the property is the object of a compulsory purchase order; or
- the property is pulled down or so damaged so that its value is materially depreciated.

The loan offer should be read through carefully and legal advice sought regarding its contents, with particular attention paid to any of the special conditions.

On signing the letter of loan offer with the solicitor, a borrower will also have to sign a number of other documents, including:

- the mortgage documents, which are later registered;
- an authority allowing the solicitor to act on the borrower's behalf; and
- a family home declaration confirming the status of the property under the various pieces of family law legislation.

After the letter of loan offer, the most important document that should be read through by the borrower is the loan terms and conditions. Some of the mortgage institutions compile a separate booklet, which is written as clearly as possible in plain English and should be read through. Other institutions print the mortgage conditions in the mortgage documents, which are then registered in the Land Registry and are phrased entirely in legal language.

1:4 STAGE PAYMENTS AND MORTGAGES

Some purchasers will be asked to buy a house through a building agreement (*see* **Chapter 4, Deposits and Contracts, para 4:4.1**), which may stipulate that the house is to be paid through stage payments. A stage payment is a payment made to a builder during the course of construction and before the house has been completed. If this is the case, purchasers should inform their mortgage lender that they will need the mortgage to be paid in stage payments. This is so that the mortgage lender can include that arrangement in its letter of loan offer. The mortgage lender will also seek a report at each stage of construction from the architect who is overseeing the construction of the property.

As each stage is completed, for instance at first-floor level, the architect will inspect the property and issue a certificate to the mortgage lender. As each subsequent stage is completed, further stage payments are requested from the mortgage lender until the house is completely built. The purchaser's solicitors should then request the stage payment from the mortgage lender. The only complication that may arise is whether or not the stage payment is covered under the HomeBond scheme (*see* **Chapter 8, Protection from Building Defects, para 8:6**). If not, the site will have to be purchased outright. If the property is not covered by any such scheme, then the mortgage lenders will insist that the site is purchased by the borrower before any stage payments are paid to the builder so that any construction which is covered by a stage payment will be contained on a site which the borrower, and through them the mortgage lender, owns. The practice is the same as if the person was building a house on his or her own site.

Before the first stage payment is paid the mortgage documents will have to have been signed by the borrowers. The borrowers' solicitors should also proceed to register the site and mortgages. The borrowers will be expected to discharge the necessary outlays at this stage. Some solicitors will require that their bill of costs, including their professional fee, be paid when the first stage payment is drawn down, as most of the necessary work will have been undertaken by the solicitors. The remaining stage payments will then be drawn down on a property which is registered in the borrowers' name. Therefore, the borrower is protected against any possible actions which may be taken by, for example, trade creditors.

To draw down the first stage payment the borrower must ensure that all of the necessary documents are in order and have been lodged with the mortgage lender. These would include:

- the house insurance policy on the property;
- the life insurance policy on the borrowers;
- the direct debit mandate to discharge the monthly repayments;

- evidence of earnings;
- evidence of address;
- copy of identification (such as a drivers licence or passport); and
- the valuation on the property carried out by the mortgage lender's valuer together with any fees due, such as the valuation fee or mortgage indemnity bond.

The solicitors for the borrower must also ensure that closing searches are carried out against the property and against the developer and the borrowers.

For subsequent draw downs, a stage payment request must be sent to the mortgage lender along with a stage payment certificate — completed by the supervising architect or engineer — and the cheque requisition form. Once the site has been transferred to the borrower, there is no need for any additional legal work to be done for any of the subsequent draw downs. If the site has not been transferred to the borrower, the first stage payment and subsequent stage payments must be covered under the HomeBond in order to protect the payments being made to the builder. Stage payment certificates are also required if the borrower is buying a house that is not covered under the HomeBond scheme, or where the house is being built by direct labour or under a once-off building contract.

Final stage payments are only issued once the architect or supervising engineer has certified that the property complies with planning permission and building regulations. If the property is covered under the HomeBond scheme, then the final HomeBond certificate, called the HB11, is required. The fire insurance cover on the property will have to be increased to take into account the fact that the property has been completed and is ready for occupation. However, most fire insurance policies are taken out for the full value of the property when the first stage payment is made and are rarely taken out on a piecemeal basis.

It is important for borrowers to realise that they have an obligation to insure the property against any risks that the mortgage lender may stipulate. At a minimum this would be taken to include fire insurance. The mortgage lender is usually not under any obligation to ensure that the insurance cover which is in place is adequate. Mortgage lenders can require borrowers to submit a copy of the receipt for the insurance premium and can require that the interest of the mortgage lender is noted on the insurance policy.

2 NEW HOUSE GRANT

2:1 INTRODUCTION

The Housing (Miscellaneous Provisions) Act 1979 introduced a grant for the construction of new houses, flats and maisonettes, where certain conditions are met. The provision was enacted in order to facilitate the construction of new houses and, at the time, to give a boost to the construction industry.

The current grant is €3,800 (£3,000) or €12,190 (£9,600) in the case of a dwelling situated on certain islands off the west and south coasts of Ireland.

2:2 ELIGIBILITY

The new house grant is sometimes referred to as a "first time buyers grant". However, this is not strictly correct, as the applicant need not be a first time buyer of property in the strict sense. The eligibility requirements are that:

- the house, flat or maisonette must be new, built in accordance with good building practice, with a floor area (in the case of a house) that does not exceed 125 square metres and not less than 38 square metres;

- the grant must not have been previously applied for by either party in the case of married persons and the dwelling must be used as the applicants' normal place of residence;

- the applicant must not have previously purchased or built another dwelling in Ireland or abroad as a residence for occupation; and

- the house must be built by a contractor who is registered for VAT.

Where a house is being built on the applicant's own site, the VAT-registered work must not be less than €19,000. More than one VAT-registered contractor can contribute to making up this threshold.

2:3 DOCUMENTS REQUIRED

New house owners need to fill in an application form from the Department of the Environment and Local Government, based in Ballina, Co. Mayo. The details to be included on the form are:

1. The full names of the applicant and the spouse of the applicant;
2. The occupations of the applicant(s);
3. The address of the property for which the grant is being applied.
4. A floor area certificate, if it has been issued. If a floor area certificate has not been issued for the dwelling, then the following should be submitted with the application:
   (a) a site location map;
   (b) a house plan;
   (c) elevation and section drawings; and
   (d) specifications for the dwelling;
5. The final grant of planning permission; and
6. A copy of a written contract and a VAT invoice for the VAT-registered work.

The contract for either the purchase or the construction of the dwelling should be certified as a true copy by the applicant's solicitor and enclosed with the application form. The form needs to be signed by the applicant before a Peace Commissioner, a Commissioner for Oaths or a Notary Public. In cases where these people are not available, the form may be signed before a member of the Garda Síochána or a member of the clergy.

The remaining parts of the application consist of a certificate from the relevant Inspector of Taxes. The applicant(s) must fill in the relevant details, including:

- their tax numbers;
- the tax numbers of the main builder; and
- the builders' C2 certificate number or the number for the builders' tax clearance certificate.

This certificate must be forwarded to the Inspector of Taxes. The Inspector of Taxes will certify that:

(a) the applicant has not applied for income tax relief in respect of interest paid on money that was borrowed to purchase or build a dwelling;
(b) the tax number is correct; and
(c) a previous application has not been made under that tax number.

2:4 PAYMENT OF THE GRANT AND SPECIAL EXEMPTIONS

Once the dwelling is finished and is occupied by the applicant, a certificate of provisional approval is forwarded to the applicant by the Department of the Environment and Local Government. Payment may be claimed by signing the declaration on this certificate. The Department may send an inspector to check the dwelling to ensure that all conditions of the scheme have been complied with. Payment is then made to the applicant by cheque or through the applicants' bank account. Payment of the grant, however, does not warrant that the dwelling has been completed in accordance with planning permission or has been constructed in compliance with building regulations.

A special exemption may be granted in the case of a new house that has been suitably designed or specially adapted to meet the needs of a disabled member of the household. The exemption may be given in relation to the floor area limit, or in respect of the requirement that the applicant should not have previously purchased or built a dwelling. A new house grant may also be allowed to a person whose marriage has been dissolved or annulled by an order of court or who has been separated under an order of court or by way of a deed of separation. A grant cannot be paid to a person who is not separated "in writing" from his or her spouse, and legal advice should be obtained as early as possible in order to ensure eligibility for the grant.

A new house grant may also be given to a person whose house has been damaged by fire, explosion or by an act of God, and where it is more reasonable for a new house to be constructed than for the existing one to be repaired, and where a refusal to pay the grant would cause undue hardship.

3 BUYING A SECOND-HAND HOUSE

3:1 GET A SURVEY DONE

Anyone interested in purchasing second-hand property should enquire from the auctioneer or the person selling the property how old it is. The basic law relating to second-hand property is *caveat emptor*, or "buyer beware". In other words, the law assumes, to a certain degree, that the buyer was aware of the condition of the property before buying it. Over time, the law has tried to protect purchasers of property, but that level of protection is mainly limited to instances of fraud or mistake. In most cases, if the seller of the property does not disclose a problem, for instance damp, to the purchaser, there is usually very little in law that the purchaser can do in relation to the seller.

3:1.1 Choosing the sureyor

It is important to have a survey conducted by an experienced and competent surveyor, architect or engineer. It is also advisable to ensure that the surveyor used has professional indemnity insurance and is a member of a professional body.

3:1.2 Type of survey

The age of the property will determine the type of survey which needs to be conducted. Some surveyors will insist on taking up floorboards and drilling holes into certain walls as well as climbing up into the attic space. While some properties will require a great deal of surveying work, most of the building constructed within the past 15 to 20 years will have been constructed according to modern techniques and practices and according to the Building Regulations.

If the property has been built within the past five years, then it may still be covered by the HomeBond scheme (*see* **Chapter 8: Protection from Building Defects, para 8:6**) or by the builder's indemnity. If the property is nearly 10 years old, the protection of the HomeBond will be coming to an end, as may be the statutory period of limitation for actions against the original builder (*see* **Chapter 8: Protection from Building Defects, para 8:4**).

3:1.3 Foundations

Any survey should include an examination of the foundations and surrounding site to ensure that the property is not subsiding. Using a local surveyor will ensure that knowledge of the area will be applied to the survey. While coal mining, which could this cause subsidence, is not a common feature of the landscape in Ireland, flooding is, and local surveyors will be able to point out which properties are more susceptible to flooding. Getting an Ordnance Survey map of the area will also help in identifying areas that may be prone to flooding. Examining the property itself will also provide some clues. Cracks in the walls may be simple plasterwork cracks, but could also have resulted from subsidence or some major structural defect. If they are obvious, they need to be checked out. It is also advisable to ask for a copy of the Land Registry map, as it may show flood plains and marshy areas that existed before the construction of the property. If necessary, ask the owner whether any work was carried out on the property to prevent flooding or subsidence or whether any claim was made on an insurance policy for it.

3:1.4 Dampness and woodwork

Woodwork will need particular attention, especially if the property is an old one, as rot may have set in. Always remember to check the condition of the doors and windows, especially on the outside, and be very suspicious of any recent painting, which may have covered over remedial work. The smell of fresh paint inside the property should also set off alarm bells, as it may be indicate that the property has a problem with damp.

Potential buyers should also be aware that certain doors and windows may not be replaced with modern doors or windows if the property is a listed building or has features that may be restricted under Planning Regulations. Always ensure that the survey includes an examination of the external doors and windows. Also ensure that the surveyor checks any wooden stairs and bannisters. The roof should be examined if the property is over 25 or 30 years old to ensure that the supporting timbers are still in good condition. The attic space in most terraced houses should always be checked — in the past it was the practice not to continue with the blockwork or brickwork to the top of the roof, thus presenting both a fire hazard and a security risk.

Some houses built between the World Wars were constructed using mass concrete that was not insulated and may not have been properly damp proofed. Damp proofing is particularly important as damp rooms are extremely hard to maintain and may cause serious health problems for some people. If the walls of a house were not damp proofed, ask why. Also, find out how much it would cost to carry out damp proofing. The answer to that question alone may prompt a potential buyer to move on to another property.

3:1.5 Check boundaries

Always ask a surveyor to check the boundaries of the property by referring to a title map or Land Registry map. While the boundary lines on a Land Registry map are indicative, they are not conclusive and problems sometimes arise through simple mistakes. In one case a local authority had incorrectly mapped a housing estate, with the result that two properties were mapped as one. The mistake was not noticed until one of the houses came to be sold and one of the solicitors pointed out that the map seemed to show a larger property than the standard terraced house.

In the case of second-hand houses built on their own sites, rather than in a housing estate, it is important to check where the septic tank and percolation areas are on the site. Septic tanks should be contained within the site itself, but it may happen that the tank and the percolation area are both outside the site. Finding the septic tank may in itself pose problems if the area has been grassed over and covered over time. If it has, then the tank was probably never properly emptied, an added expense when the property is purchased and the buyer moves into it.

In cases where the property is in a town or other built-up area, the seller should, if the standard Law Society of Ireland contracts are used, disclose any disputes with neighbouring property owners or others.' If the standard contracts are not being used, the potential buyer should make enquires from the seller. The seller is bound to give a correct answer and is then bound by that answer. In certain cases, the boundaries of a property are not clear and sometimes the exact boundary line has been lost in time. If necessary, have the exact site pegged out and agreed and always err on the side of caution. A few feet lost to no man's land is sometimes a small price to pay. If the boundaries are not agreed, they could become disputed, and the buyer should beware that boundary disputes are notoriously difficult cases to bring to court.

In some cases the boundary walls or fences may not belong to the property and may in fact be located on another person's land. The potential purchaser should be aware of this so that no disputes result from any misunderstandings in the future.

3:1.6 Planning searches and issues

Anyone wishing to purchase property would be well advised to consult the local development plan of the local authority in whose functional area the property is located. The purpose of consulting the development plan is to ascertain whether the property is, or is going to be, affected by a compulsory purchase order for some purpose, for example road widening. Every five years or so, the local planning authority adopts a new development plan, which contains its proposals for road widening or the construction of new roads. The development plan will also indicate the areas zoned for exclusive residential use, for light industrial or mixed use, for agricultural use only, and for heavy industrial use.

3:1.6.1 Where to find the development plans

Development plans are generally available at local libraries and are always available for consultation during normal office hours at the offices of the planning authority. The development plan consists of a large booklet detailing the planning area region by region and outlines the general underlying planning and development rules for the area. The plan will also contain a large number of maps which will have to be read in conjunction with one another in order to ascertain if the plans will have any impact on a property.

3:1.6.2 Planning permission information

Sometimes the property in which the potential purchaser is interested will already have the benefit of a planning permission. It would be wise to consult the planning file relating to the property, as the file will contain all of the correspondence relating to the issue of the planning permission and any objections which the planning authority may have received, and which the vendor is under no obligation to disclose in the contracts or to any solicitor acting for the purchaser. If the purchaser has any plans for the property after purchase, then an examination of the planning file must be carried out. Always telephone the planning authority office to ensure that the file will be available, as some planning authorities require some time to search for the file and make it available for inspection. The Planning Authorities were under no obligation to provide copies of anything contained in a planning permission up to the enactment of the Planning and Development Act 2000. Therefore, expect to spend some time writing everything down and bring a copy of the area map so that notes can be made on it, as some files still cannot be copied. Planning permissions and planning files created after the Planning and Development Act 2000 can be copied and purchased from the Planning Authorities.

Do not assume that you can add extensions to the property — always check with an architect or with the local authority to see whether they will be allowed under the Planning Regulations. Since June 2001, householders will be able to extend their properties by up to 40 square metres, subject to a number of restrictions. Also, do not assume that the property may be extended or altered by adding, for example, an additional window to the gable end of the property or toward the front of the house. Most internal alterations will be classed as exempted development under the Local Government (Planning and Development) Acts, but the addition of extra windows to the side and front of buildings are not.

3:2 HOUSE CONTENTS

3:2.1 Contents included in the sale of the property

When purchasing second-hand property it is common for some house contents to be included in the purchase price. The estate agent or auctioneer will try to ensure that both the seller and purchaser are aware of the contents that are being sold with the property. The general rule is that if you need to use a screwdriver to remove it, then it should come with the property. This includes lights and fittings, showers, shower trays, cookers, fridges and freezers. Cookers, fridges and freezers are generally assumed to come with the property if they are fitted into the kitchen but are not included if they are free standing. It is advisable to check with the estate agent or auctioneer as to whether items in the kitchen are included.

3:2.2 Contents not included in the sale

If the contents are not included in the sale of the property, both parties will need to agree on the prices of any items that the purchaser wishes to retain. The contents are not included in the deed of transfer or conveyance as the consideration being paid for the property for stamp duty purposes, but the price of the contents is included with the price being paid for the property to decide on the relevant rate of stamp duty. For instance, if the total purchase price, including the contents, attracts a 9 per cent rate of stamp duty, the stamp duty is payable on the price less the value of the contents. Purchasers should also enquire as to whether any of the contents included in the sale of the property or being bought from the seller are being purchased by the seller by way of hire-purchase agreements — a common occurrence, especially for goods like couches and electrical items.

3:2.3 Garden furniture

Garden furniture may not be included in the property for sale and enquiries should be made from the seller if the garden is well stocked with furniture, and indeed plants, as the seller may intend to take some of the plants away on closing.

4 LEGAL CONTRACTS AND DEPOSITS

4:1 STATUE OF FRAUDS (IRELAND) ACT 1695

Once a purchaser has decided to purchase a property, care must be taken to avoid making a mistake in the way in which the bid is made and the contract is neogtiated. The legal definition of a contract for the sale or purchase of land is contained in section 2 of the Statute of Frauds (Ireland) Act 1695, which provides that:

> "... *no action shall be brought whereby to charge ... any person ... upon any contract of sale of lands, tenements or hereditaments, or any interest in or concerning them ... unless the agreement upon which such action shall be brought, or some memorandum or note thereof shall be in writing and signed by the party to be charged therewith, or some other person thereunto by him lawfully authorised.*"

In effect, this means that for there to be a valid contract in law for the sale of any interest in land, there must be something in writing that is signed by the person against whom the contract is to be enforced. There is, in fact, strictly no requirement for a deposit to be paid; but for a contract to be enforceable there must be consideration (something of value exchanged between parties to the contract). If a deposit is paid by paper (*i.e.* by cheque), paying it may provide evidence in writing that payment has taken place, indicating that there is a binding contract.

The most important point for a purchaser to take from the Statute of Frauds is that a binding contract can exist if the purchaser signs something in writing promising to purchase a property. Unless that contract is framed properly or carefully, the purchaser may be faced with buying a house without having a survey done, or even without having arranged a mortgage.

4:2 DEPOSITS

4:2.1 The booking deposit

If a purchaser gives an auctioneer a deposit and is given a receipt for the deposit, then a binding agreement or contract exists not only to purchase the property but also to sell the property. Thereafter, the practice is that purhcasers provide auctioneers with a booking deposit, which is merely an indication that the purchaser is willing to proceed with the deal. The auctioneer takes the booking deposit and either holds onto it until closing or hands it over to the solicitors for the vendor. A booking deposit, or a deposit of any kind, should under no circumstances be handed to the vendor. In fact, no deposit of any kind should be handed over to the vendor. A deposit can be forwarded to the solicitor acting for the vendor as, in law, the solicitor holds on to the deposit as stakeholder or trustee. In law, the money is still the property of the purchaser until the contract is completed, unless the contract provides otherwise.

A booking deposit is refundable and can be demanded back by the purchaser at any time before the contracts are signed. After the contracts are signed the booking deposit forms part of the contract deposit and cannot be automatically refunded to the purchaser.

Once the booking deposit has been paid, the purchaser should obtain a receipt for it. The purchaser must ensure that the receipt clearly states that the sale is "subject to contract" or "headed contract denied". Another form of words may be used, such as "subject to title". This ensures that a valid contract under the Statute of Frauds has not been made and that the valid and binding contract will come into existence later.

4:2.2 The deposit

If a booking deposit is paid, it forms part of the usual 10 per cent deposit which is paid to the solicitors for the vendor on the signing of the contracts. A deposit always has to be paid when the purchaser signs the contract. There is no particular reason why the deposit is 10 per cent; in fact 20 or 30 years ago the deposit was more likely to be 20 or even 50 per cent. The figure of 10 per cent is merely a rule of practice and can be varied by agreement between the vendor and purchaser. This rule of practice also means that the vendor will have a substantial sum to claim against the purchaser should he or she default on the contract or break the contract in some way. In practice, the auctioneer or estate agent will also use the booking deposit as a part payment against fees and expenses for selling the property.

Once the booking deposit has been paid, purchasers should contact a solicitor as well as their mortgage company, as the closing of the sale would usually be scheduled for eight weeks after the signing of the contract. Purchasers should discuss with their solicitor any special conditions that may have to be included in the contracts in order to facilitate a "risk-free" purchase (*see* **para 4:3.1**). Purchasers should, in fact, have already have made contact with a mortgage company in order to make sure that they qualify for a mortgage and that the purchase will be properly financed. The deposit stipulated in the contract will be paid to the solicitors when the contracts are signed.

4:2.3 Multiple deposits

There may be two sets of contracts for new houses being built by a developer in a housing estate, or by a private developer buying sites for development later on. One contract will deal with the sale of the site and the other with the construction of the house. The contract dealing with the construction of the house is called the building agreement. Deposits will be payable on each of these contracts and will usually add up to an overall 10 per cent of the purchase price. The deposit on the building agreement may be treated differently to the deposit on the purchase of the site, as the developer may use the deposit toward the construction of the house. The contracts must be carefully examined to see if this is the case. The recommended best practice is that deposits are not handed over to the vendor until completion, although there will be some exceptions to this rule, particularly where the contract is for the purchase of a house to be built in stages with the stage payments being paid to the builder (*see* **Chapter 1: Financing your House, para 1:4**).

4:3 CONTRACTS AND SPECIAL CONDITIONS

4:3.1 Special conditions

The term "special conditions" refers to any condition of sale that is peculiar to the sale or purchase of the property. For instance, if there are some contents included in the sale that were specially agreed between the parties, then that fact would be included in the contracts. In the standard Law Society of Ireland contracts, the latest edition of which was issued in 2002, the special conditions are contained before the general conditions and just after the legal description of the property.

4:3.2 Examples of purchasers' conditions

If a purchaser intends to get a mortgage to purchase the property, it is advisable to put in a special condition in the contract allowing the purchaser to obtain a mortgage so that he or she could withdraw from the purchase if the mortgage is not approved by a financial institution. The special condition can also be worded so as to allow the purchaser to withdraw from the purchase if the financial institution gives a mortgage subject to terms and conditions, some of which the purchaser may not be able to comply with. One example may be that the letter of loan offer from the bank or building society is conditional on the borrower renting out one of the rooms in the house. If the purchaser believes that he or she cannot comply with that condition, then he or she will not get the mortgage and consequently will not be able to purchase the property.

4:3.3 Examples of vendors' conditions

Sometimes it is the vendor who inserts a special condition into the contract. This is especially the case where the vendor is a property developer, or where the sale of a second-hand property depends on the completion of other legal work. A vendor may also insert a condition that the sale is dependent on the vendor being able to purchase another house within a defined period, or indeed the purchaser being able to sell his or her house before completing the purchase of the new house.

One common special condition for contracts involving the sale of second-hand houses is a condition stating that the purchaser, by signing the contracts, is accepting the property in its current state and condition. If this is the case, then the purchaser should obtain a survey on the property before signing the contracts, because the property may have some defect or fault. The purchaser, should also ask the vendor why the condition was inserted and also ask specific questions regarding the house. The rule is that the vendor will be bound by the answers given, unless the vendor insists on standing over the written contract and does not bind himself or herself to any answers or assurances given. This would take the form of another special condition, stating that the vendor is not bound by any assurances or statements made up to the signing of the contracts. The buyer should be wary of all such special conditions.

4:3.4 Checking special conditions before signing

Once the solicitor for the purchaser receives the contract from the solicitor for the vendor, the purchaser should ask to be sent a copy of it before making an appointment to sign the contracts. This will give the purchaser an opportunity to examine the contracts and the special conditions, as well as to check any map that may be attached to the contracts. If a map has not been included, it is advisable to seek one for the property. The special conditions must be examined before the contract is signed. Very often purchasers query the conditions in the contract after the contract has been signed and exchanged, after which nothing can be done. In the vast majority of contracts for new houses, the developer's solicitors will have inserted a number of common special conditions into each of the contracts for each of the houses being sold. Most of these conditions will relate to the fact that developers have sent out two forms of contracts. One relates to the sale of the site upon which the house will be built, while the second contract is a building agreement contracting to build the house for the purchaser.

4:4 BUILDING AGREEMENTS AND SITE CONTRACTS

The basic idea behind the issue of two different contracts for the purchase of one house is that the site is sold under one contract and the house is built under another contract. In some cases, the person who sells the site may be different from the one who builds the house. An example of this is where a private landowner decides to sell his land to a developer on a per site basis, for instance, at €25,000 per site, as well as an overall premium of, say, €100,000. The developer contracts to buy, or rather sell on, the site and to build the houses and finish the estate. The owner of the land contracts to sell the site on to whoever wants to purchase the house, in a way — selling it twice. The eventual purchaser is often unaware of the existence of the landowner until the contracts are issued.

Both contracts are signed together and are part of the same deal. However, in some key aspects they are very different. The contract for the sale of the site deals entirely with the parcel of land on which the house will be built. It will deal with the title to the property and refers to the easements, rights and privileges which go with the property. The building agreement is the vehicle through which the house is constructed and contains the warranties, terms and conditions relating to the building of the house. If any problems arise with the house after it has been constructed, it is to the building agreement that lawyers will turn to see what kind of guarantees have been given.

4:4.1 Building agreement

The building agreement is, in effect, a contract to build or complete a building project, with the purchaser called "the employer" and the developer called "the builder." The building agreement will state that the purchaser of the house employs the developer as a builder to construct the house according to the plans and specifications tendered, within a certain time period and for a stated amount of money. The standard building agreement used by the Law Society of Ireland provides that the builder may not without the prior consent of the purchaser assign the contract to any other person, or in other words, have someone else take over the building of the house. This, however, does not apply to the practice of sub-contracting, whereby the main builder gets in specialists to carry out certain works, such as installing kitchens.

4:4.1.1 Plans and specifications

The purchaser will have been given the plans and specifications for the house when the contracts are first issued to the purchaser's solicitor. The builder or developer must construct the house according to the plans which are, in effect, agreed upon between the parties. This is because the purchaser, by making a bid on the property, will have either seen the plans for the house or inspected a showhouse. If the purchaser has not seen the plans or inspected the showhouse before making a bid, he or she should inspect them carefully when they are issued with the contracts. In every case, the plans and specifications should be double-checked before the contracts are sent back to the solicitors for the developer.

4:4.1.2 Altering the building agreement

The building agreement can be altered, for instance, by changing the closing date or making alterations to the plans or specifications, by agreement between the parties. If a purchaser wants to make changes to the plans, he or she should approach the builder and agree the changes by marking them on the plans or specifications, and by signing or initialling the changes. As a matter of practice, any purchaser should try to make all of the necessary changes to the house as early as possible and discuss all of the changes at one time so as to minimise disruption to the building schedule.

4:4.1.3 Payment

The building agreement will also outline the method of payment for the construction of the house and the expected time it will take to finish the construction. A building agreement will also state that if the purchaser does not make the necessary payments on time, there may be interest or penalties charged. It will also set out how the payments or stage payments are requested and how they become payable.

4:4.1.4 Repair of defects

Crucially, the building agreement will also stipulate the time period during which the purchaser must ensure that the builder carries out any remedial repairs to major and minor defects. The most common time period, or maximum period of time in which one is permitted to make a complaint for minor defects, is six months from the date of completion. The common time period allowed to raise any problems regarding major defects is between seven and 10 years. Most solicitors acting for purchasers will try to ensure that the building agreement will at least contain the same protection as contained in the HomeBond scheme (*see* **Chapter 8, Protection from Building Defect, para 8:6**). On the other hand, builders will try to limit their liability to six years, or less if possible.

Building agreements may also contain a price-variation clause, which is a clause allowing a change in the price of the construction of the house if the prices of materials change or if there is a change in the rate of VAT charged. It is advisable that the price-variation clause be deleted from building agreements unless specifically agreed upon between the parties.

4:4.1.5 Dispute resolution

The building agreement may contain a clause providing that any dispute between the parties be put to arbitration, along with details of how the arbitration is to be carried out and by whom. Arbitration is generally considered a more effective way of ending or solving contractual disputes and may be less expensive and time consuming than court action. This may be an important point to remember if any problems arise, as the most common reason for delay during the arbitration procedure is the fact that the parties did not go to arbitration quickly enough or that they did not appoint an arbitrator at the first opportunity.

4:4.1.6 Closing date

A building agreement will generally contain a clause that will try to outline the expected closing date. The building agreement will generally stipulate that the closing date will be six months from the date of signing of the agreement. It will go on to provide that that time may be extended by notice to the purchaser by the builder, so long as the reason provided for the extension is a reasonable one and all reasonable efforts have been made to complete the construction of the house. Generally, the purchaser will want to have the house completed as quickly as possible but, while the contract may appear to state that the house must be completed within six months, almost all contracts will allow the builder to extend that period.

4:4.2 Contract for the site

The contract for the sale or purchase of the site will set out who its owners are and the price to be paid for it. The monies for the site are paid at the same time as the first stage payments under the building agreement. This is because a purchaser should be the owner of the land on which the house is being built when any money is handed over to the builder or land owner, unless a HomeBond agreement is in place and the monies handed over are covered by the HomeBond scheme (*see* **Chapter 8, Protection from Building Defect, para 8:6**). If the purchaser did not insist on becoming the legal owner of the site, then the builder would receive payment for the work done on the house and would still retain ownership of the site. If the builder then became insolvent or bankrupt, the site would pass to the creditors, or the receivers, and the purchaser would not have legal ownership of the site, only of the bricks and mortar on the land.

The contract will state that it is tied with or connected to the building agreement and that one stands on top of the other. However, it is as yet unsettled in law as to whether a builder can insist on taking back a site if the entire purchase price is not paid, that is, the total price for the site and for the building agreement. A recent decision of the High Court in relation to the Unfair Terms in Consumer Contracts Regulations 1995, and the European Directive upon which it is based, has meant that builders or developers need to be careful about the type of contracts they issue. The Court held that builders or developers should not be allowed to have a clause in a building agreement that would allow the builder to take back the site, or rescind the agreement, within 14 days of demanding the instalments or stage payments. The Court also held that builders should not be allowed to restrict the right of employers (or house purchasers) to raise snag lists or make a claim or demand in respect of the materials used or the workmanship or of the size or measurements of the site. Likewise, a clause in the contract for the site or the building agreement stating that a purchaser had to give notice of any defects in the property before taking possession of the property or before paying the balance of the contract price was held to be unfair and, therefore, illegal. The practice of restricting the purchaser to one snag list was also held to be unfair, as was a provision reserving the right to modify materials or specifications and varying the dimensions of the site and building during construction. This can only be done if both the builder and the purchaser agree prior to any change in the materials, specifications or dimensions, unless the changes are reasonable.

The High Court decided that instalment, stage or interim payments (all meaning the same thing) should not exceed the extent and value of works that have been carried out to date and set out the maximum percentages that can be sought at the relevant stages. It also restricted the right of builders to charge interest on late payments.

The High Court stated that the maximum booking deposit should be 4 per cent, the contract deposit should be no more than 11 per cent, and the interim payments for joist, roof levels and internal plastering should not be more than 25 per cent for each stage, which levels at 10 per cent on completion.

4:4.2.1 Completion of housing estates

The contract for the sale of the site will stipulate the time-frame in which the rest of the estate is expected to be completed. Most contracts, however, state that the sale or purchase of the house is not dependent on the completion of the entire estate. They state that the developer only has to complete the development, that is the housing estate, within a reasonable time.

5 STAMP DUTY

5:1 INTRODUCTION

Stamp duty is a tax which is charged on certain documents, such as deeds of conveyance, mortgage documents, share transfers, cheques and so on. Stamp duty is not a tax on property directly, but is an indirect tax charged on the document transferring legal ownership of land (ownership of land cannot transfer from one person to another unless there is evidence in writing).

5:2 RATES FOR RESIDENTIAL PROPERTY

Residential property is classed in section 1 of the Stamp Duties Consolidation Act 1999 as a building which was used or was suitable for use as a dwelling at the date of its purchase. This definition also includes the curtilage of the residential property for up to one acre. The curtilage of a house includes lands ordinarily used for the benefit or enjoyment of the owners of a property and would include a garden, garden shed, garage and so on.

5:2.1 First time buyers

The stamp duty rates on residential property depend on the status of the purchaser. A first time purchaser is a person or persons who:

- has not on any previous occasion, either individually or jointly, purchased or built a house in Ireland or abroad; and

- purchases the property which is occupied by the purchaser, or a person on his or her behalf, as his or her only or principal place of residence; and

- does not obtain rent from the property for a period of five years from the date of purchase.

The last criterion does not included the rent-a-room scheme allowed by the Government (*see* **para 5:4**).

The stamp duty rules also allow a spouse in a marriage that has ended by way of divorce, nullity, judicial separation or deed of separation to be classed as a first time buyer.

The first time buyer rates are as follows:

Value of Property	Rate of stamp duty
under €190,500	no stamp duty
between €190,501 and €254,000	3%
between €254,001 and €317,500	3.75%
between €317,501 and €381,000	5.5%
between €381,001 and €635,000	7.5%
over €635,000	9%

It should also be noted that, where applicable, the VAT element of the purchase price should be excluded from the chargeable consideration. VAT is charged on the building agreement element of new-house purchases.

5:2.2 Owner-occupiers

An owner-occupier is a person who purchases a house intending to occupy it as his or her only or principal place of residence. No rent should be obtained from the property for a period of five years from the date of purchase. Again, the rent-a-room scheme is exempted from the definition of rental income, and applies to the letting of furnished accommodation in part of a house on or after April 6, 2001.

A clawback of stamp duty relief or reduced rate applies if rent is obtained from the letting of the house (a "clawback" is a demand for payment by the Revenue of the stamp duty that would have been due). This relief or reduced rate is payable on the date on which the first rent is received from the property. The applicable rate will be the rate of stamp duty that would have applied when the house was originally bought and not any later stamp duty rate, such as the prevailing rate of stamp duty when the deed is presented for stamping.

For owner-occupiers, the rates of stamp duty are the same as for investors who are purchasing new houses or apartments, and are as follows:

Value of property	Rate of stamp duty
less than €127,000	no stamp duty
between €127,001 and €190,500	3%
between €190,501 and €254,000	4%
between €254,001 and €317,500	5%
between €317,501 and €381,000	6%
between €381,001 and €635,000	7.5%
over €635,000	9%

5:2.3 Investors

An investor is a person who does not qualify as either a first time buyer or as an owner-occupier. Any person buying a second home, including a holiday home, is classed as an investor, even if no rent is received for the property or there is no intention of selling the property in the future for a profit.

For investors, the rate of stamp duty from June 15, 2000 was 9 per cent for both new and second-hand houses, regardless of how much was paid for the property. From February 27, 2001 the rate of stamp duty was reduced for new houses bought by investors. For investors in second-hand property — either houses or apartments — the rate is 9 per cent for all property purchased before December 6, 2001. The Finance Act 2002 changed the rates for investors purchasing new and second-hand property. The rates for new houses and apartments are as follows:

Value of property	Rate of stamp duty
up to €127,000	no stamp duty payable
between €127,000 and €190,500	3%
between €190,501 and €254,000	4%
between €254,001 and €317,500	5%
between €317,501 and €381,000	6%
between €381,001 and €635,000	7.5%
over €635,000	9%

For all second-hand property, the rates are the same as for new properties from December 6, 2001.

Where the property being purchased is composed of part residential and part non-residential, the stamp duty rates are applied to each separate component. That is, the residential part of the property is valued and taxed as above, while the non-residential part is taxed along the same lines as property with no house or apartment on it at all. An apportionment form is filled out and forwarded to the Revenue when the deed is being stamped.

5:3 NON-RESIDENTIAL PROPERTY

Any deed of transfer, conveyance or assignment that sells or disposes of property with a market value of less than €6,350 is exempt from any stamp duty. The rates are as follows:

Value of property	Rate of stamp duty
between €6,350 and €12,700	1%
between €12,700 and €19,050	2%
between €19,050 and €31,750	3%
between €31,750 and €63,500	4%
between €63,500 and €76,200	5%
over €76,200	6%

The rates are progressive and not cumulative, so a property valued at €50,000 would attract 4 per cent stamp duty.

5:4 RELIEFS FROM STAMP DUTY

- Where a property is being sold or has been given to someone who is related to the vendor, the rate of stamp duty is half of the duty that would otherwise be payable and is known as consanguinity relief. The degree of relationship is governed by law but includes most relatives who would be regarded as family members.

- Other reliefs are available against stamp duty and include young trained farmer relief and woodlands relief. The transfer of a site from parent to child is not liable to stamp duty since

December 6, 2000, provided the site is valued at under €254,000.

• The rent-a-room scheme is a form of stamp duty relief as well as an income tax relief, and allows an owner who resides in the property to rent out a room to another person without potentially attracting stamp duty. It also allows an exemption from income tax on gross income up to €7,618. If the rental income exceeds €7,618, then the full amount is taxable.

5:5 STAMP DUTY AND MORTGAGES

For some purchasers an additional stamp duty on the mortgage may be charged on top of the house purchase. At present there is no stamp duty on any mortgage below €254,000. For any mortgages above that threshold, the rate of duty is €1 per €1,000 borrowed or covered under the mortgage. The duty is charged on the entire amount borrowed. For example if the mortgage is €300,000, then the stamp duty will be €300.

5:6 PAYING THE STAMP DUTY

Stamp duty is payable within 28 days of the deed of transfer or convey-ance being signed by any party. The stamp duty is payable by the pur-chaser, in practice within a month of the closing of the purchase, and the duty is embossed on the deed of transfer or conveyance. When the deed is sent for stamping to the Revenue Commissioners, in Sullivan's Quay, Cork, or in Dublin Castle, Dublin 2, a form known as the Partic-ulars Delivered Form is also sent. The Particulars Delivered, or PD Form contains:

• a brief outline of the transaction;
• the names and addresses of the parties;
• the PPS (formerly RSI) numbers of the parties;
• the address of the property;
• the consideration, or price, which was paid for the property;
• a brief description of the property.

When the deed comes back stamped, there is a silver folio along one side on which there are the letters "PD", the currency and the amount of duty paid. If the transaction is between parties who are related, and if the purchaser is seeking consanguinity relief, the deed of transfer or conveyance must be adjudicated upon, or in order words assessed by the Revenue. Once it has been assessed and the duty paid, the foil is amended to reflect that fact. Copies of the stamped deed of transfer or conveyance should be kept in case the original is lost or destroyed.

6 COMPLETING A PURCHASE

6:1 CLOSING A SALE OR PURCHASE

The procedure relating to the closing of a sale or purchase of property has become a lot more straightforward than in the past. The previous practice was to have the solicitors for both the vendor and the purchaser present along with their clients, as well as the solicitor for the financial institution that was lending the money to the purchaser. These three-way closings are uncommon these days, and in fact are almost solely confined to large commercial transactions.

Modern closings, by and large, take place through the post or by the solicitor for the purchaser calling to the office of the solicitor for the vendor. There is generally no need for either the purchaser or the vendor to be present. If the closing takes place by post, then the solicitor for the vendor will forward the title documents or closing documents to the solicitor for the purchaser. These documents will be held in trust by the solicitor for the purchaser until the balance of the purchase monies is received and clear searches are received by the purchaser's solicitors.

6:2 CLOSING SEARCHES

Searches are conducted on closing by the solicitors for the purchaser. The searches are carried out in various government offices in Dublin. The solicitor will get a specialist company or colleagues in Dublin to go into the High Court's judgment and bankruptcy office to make sure that the vendors have not been made bankrupt, as bankrupt people may not sell property on their own behalf. The judgment office holds a record of judgements that have been registered and need to be paid prior to any property being sold. This system was developed so that any outstanding judgments would be paid before the property was sold.

Other searches have to be done in either the Land Registry or the Registry of Deeds. This is because even though the purchaser's solicitors will have received copies of the title documents, it is still possible for a charge or a judgment mortgage to be registered right up to the day of the closing of the sale. By conducting searches on the day of the closing, the purchaser's solicitors ensure that the title remains clear, as the deed of transfer will be dated on the day of closing and will take priority if any charge is lodged after that and before the purchaser registers the new deed of transfer.

Where the property being purchased is a leasehold property, as is usually the case with a flat, then searches need to be conducted in the Sheriffs Office, as leasehold property is regarded in law as being similar to chattels, that is, equipment and suchlike. Leasehold property is a lesser class of real property than freehold property, and means that a landlord holds the freehold title.

Where the vendor is registered as a company, searches need to be conducted in the Companies Office, also located in Dublin. Company law is a highly technical area of law and is somewhat complicated. Nearly every act committed by a company or taken against a company has to be registered in the Companies Office and placed on the company's permanent record. The solicitors for the purchaser will examine all the acts that appear on the Companies Office search, including any mortgages taken out by the company. The search in the Companies Office will also show whether the company has been placed in receivership or examinership and whether it has been liquidated or even dissolved. If the company has been dissolved, then it cannot sell any property, because it no longer exists and must be reinstated. A company can be dissolved for many reasons, including by the Companies Office for failure to lodge annual reports.

6:3 CLOSING DOCUMENTS

Both the sellers and buyers of property will need to sign various closing documents to complete the sale or purchase of property. Some closings will involve more closing documents than others, but generally closings will need the some or all of the following.

6:3.1 Family home declaration

If you are purchasing a property with the aid of a mortgage from either a building society or a bank, you will need to sign a family home declaration stating whether or not the property is a family home. The vendor of the property will also need to give a family home declaration on closing, or will have to ensure that his or her spouse has signed a consent to the sale prior to the contracts being signed. If the spouse also owns the proerty, both husband and wife sign a family home declaration on closing.

The family home declaration was introduced by the Family Home Protection Act 1976. The Act provides that any conveyance of property that contains the family home or part of the family home of any person, will be null and void if the prior consent of the spouse of the owner is not obtained. The term "conveyance" includes a mortgage, lease, assent, transfer, disclaimer, release and any other disposition of property. The term "family home" primarily means a dwelling in which a married couple ordinarily reside. The Act operates to protect a non-owning spouse from having the family home sold without his or her consent. If both spouses own the family home, then they both sign the family home declaration confirming that fact and confirming that the property is not the family home of any other person. There is no protection under the Act for co-habiting couples or co-habiting couples with children.

In quite a few cases the property may be the family home of other people, who may not appear to be the vendor. A good example of this is where a developer that is a limited company sells a house that has been used as the family home of one of the directors or members of the company. It would therefore be necessary for the spouse of the director to consent to the sale of the property.

Generally, a new property is not regarded in law as the family home of any person because the property has not been occupied by any married couple. Most second-hand properties will be covered under the Family Home Protection Act 1976, as a married couple will have lived in the property at some time.

6:4 DEEDS OF CONVEYANCE OR TRANSFER

6:4.1 Deeds of conveyance

The deeds of conveyance or the deeds of transfer are the legal documents which convey or transfer the property from one person to another, or to a number of other people. The term "deed of conveyance" is used to indicate that the fee simple of a property is being transferred from one person to another. (The term "fee simple" or "in fee" means that the property is held without reference to any other superior interest in the property, such as a landlord.) It usually refers to unregistered land or to lands that are not registered in the Land Registry. Deeds of conveyance are registered in the Registry of Deeds.

Where the property being purchased is a second-hand house and is registered in the Registry of Deeds, a bundle of documents will be handed over on closing. These documents are loosely referred to as "prior title". They would include the previous owners' deeds of conveyance and all of the relevant title documents associated with the property. The solicitors for the purchaser will always have received copies of the relevant prior title with the contracts.

6:4.2 Deeds of transfer

The term "deed of transfer" also refers to conveyance but relates to land registered in the Land Registry. The deed of transfer is the principal legal title document and must be signed by the vendor and the purchaser. The deed is then sent to the Revenue Commissioners for stamping and is lodged, along with other title documents and the relevant fee, in the Land Registry.

A copy of the stamped deed of transfer should always be kept so that the purchaser has a record of the transaction and can show it to any subsequent purchaser. Certain deeds of transfer may also contain conditions and covenants relating to the property. A copy of the deed of transfer should be kept so that the purchaser can, if necessary, refer to it.

For further information on titles documents, see **Chapter 7, Registering Title**.

6:5 STRUCTURAL DEFECTS INDEMNITY AND HOMEBOND

These documents are important title documents with a life span of between six and 12 years. The structural defects indemnity and Home-Bond should be kept with the title documents to the property. A copy should also be kept in case the documents need to be referred to in the event of a problem arising. For further information, see **Chapter 8, Protection from Building Defects, paras 8:5** and **8:6**.

6:6. SECTION 72 DECLARATIONS AND ASSOCIATED DECLARATIONS

A section 72 declaration is a statement confirming that the property is not affected by any right or use that is not registered in the Land Registry. It is declared before a Peace Commissioner or a Commissioner for Oaths. Although most acts or dealings in property need to be registered in the Land Registry, some uses of property do not. The section 72 declaration, which is signed by the vendors, confirms that the property is not affected by any such rights or uses.

An example of another declaration which may be included with the title documents would be a declaration regarding fishing or sporting rights that had been registered on the property in the Land Registry but no longer affect the property.

6:7 PLANNING DOCUMENTS

6:7.1 Certificate or opinion

In quite a few cases, a certificate or opinion is included with the title documents relating to planning permission. This states whether any extensions or alterations have been done on the property and is usually signed by an architect or engineer. The architect's opinion states that the property has been built in substantial compliance with the planning permission issued for the property.

6:7.2 Planning permission

The initial planning permission will also be included with the closing documents. It is important to remember that the first planning permission document which is issued to the applicant is not the final decision, but merely the approval. After the initial approval has been issued, a 30-day period is allowed for any appeal. The final decision is issued after that period has expired, and it is this document which must be placed with the title documents on closing.

Planning permissions contain a number of conditions, for example that the applicant or builder must pay over to the local authority a sum of money to cover costs related to the development, such as sewerage and water-connection charges. Larger developments attract development bonds which are used by the local authority to properly complete a development, such as an estate, in the event of the developer not doing so. It is essential that copies of the receipts for the payments stipulated by these conditions are also given to the purchaser on closing.

6:7.3 Commencement notices

Another of the planning documents required on closing is the commencement notice, which is a document forwarded to the planning authority to indicate that the property is about to be developed. A commencement notice has had to be submitted for properties constructed since the implementation of the Building Control Act 1990.

6:8 MISCELLANEOUS DOCUMENTS

The remaining closing documents handed over to the purchaser, or the purchaser's solicitors, include previous searches carried out by previous owners and receipts for the various outgoings, such as cable TV and so on, so as to prove that no monies are left owing to any service provider.

Sometimes various other documents, such as old contracts for the sale/purchase of the property, or correspondence relating to previous sales or purchases, are also handed over on closing. These documents are of little practical relevance to the purchase, unless the relevant statute of limitations period has not yet expired, *i.e.* 12 years for actions involving real property (land) and six years for negligence. An example would be where a previous solicitor was negligent in conveying property and losses were incurred within the statutory six-year period. However, this is unlikely to concern most purchasers.

7 REGISTERING TITLE

7:1 TITLE DOCUMENTS OR DEEDS

"Title documents" is the term used by practitioners to refer to all documents which are relevant to the property and which are needed in order to properly convey the property from one owner to the next. The principal title document will be the deed of transfer or the deed of conveyance which is used to transfer or convey the property from one owner to the next. However, properties may have more than one title document. Some properties could have as many as three bundles of documents and the title documents of older properties could run to several boxes.

Most purchasers buy their property with the benefit of a mortgage and so will not actually see any of their title documents until the mortgage is paid off and the documents are returned to them. Most people will leave their title documents with their solicitors or lodge them in a safe deposit box at their bank. In fact, it is always advisable to ensure that title documents are kept in a safe place at all times and that certified copies are kept separate from the original documents. Certified copies are copies of the original documents which have been certified by a solicitor or by the Land Registry to be a true copy of the originals.

It is advisable to keep copies of your title documents yourself as if you decide to sell the property while you are still paying the mortgage, then you will at least have copies to show prospective purchasers, the originals of which will be sent by the financial institution to your solicitors on their undertaking to hold the title documents pending the sale of the property. In some cases, the solicitors may hold the title documents, but most title documents are held by the financial institution.

7:2 LAND REGISTRATION

Both the sellers and buyers of property will need to sign various closing documents to complete the sale or purchase of property. In Ireland there are two centres for land registration:

1.   the Registry of Deeds; and
2.   the Land Registry.

7:2.1 Registry of Deeds

The Registry of Deeds is located in Henrietta Street, Dublin 1. This is the oldest system of land registration. Each time a property is sold or mortgaged a separate deed is drafted. These deeds form part of a long chain of title documents, starting with the "root of title". The "root of title" is either the lease, the head lease, the fee farm grant or a deed disposing of the fee simple, which is between 20 and 40 years old. In other words, it is a document which is old enough and important enough to be used as a starting point.

The document being registered in the Registry of Deeds is a synopsis of the main deed of conveyance or assignment. In the Land Registry it is the deed of transfer which is registered. It is referred to as "the memorial". A note of the registration is stamped on the front page of the deed showing the date and time the deed was registered. The conveyancer drafts up the memorial which includes:

- the names and addresses of the seller and the purchaser;
- (sometimes) the amount that was paid for the property; and
- the legal address of the property.

The legal addresses of properties registered in the Registry of Deeds in Ireland start with the street, townland, parish, barony and county and vary from the postal address used. This means that anyone who wishes to conduct a search on property can carry out a fairly accurate search in the Registry of Deeds without needed to know what the postal address is or what the postal address may have been in the past.

7:2.2 Land Registry

The second and more common type of registration is that based on the Registration of Title Act 1964 and is known as the Land Registry. Each piece or parcel of land has its own Land Certificate and folio. The Land Certificate is the main title deed or document. All properties registered in the Land Registry are kept on individual folios, which are like folders opened for each parcel of land. The first page of the folio will state where the lands are by reference to the townland, barony and county and may also state the area of the parcel either in acres or hectares. The second page of the folio will state who owns the land and how it is held, for instance by way of a joint tenancy or for life only. The third part of the folio will state the restrictions which may be placed on the land as well as any charges, such as mortgages, which may be registered on the land. A map, or "fileplan", is also available and shows the extent of the lands on a large-scale map. However, the boundaries on the Land Registry map or fileplan merely indicate where the boundary may be or where it has been indicated in the past – they are not final or conclusive.

Whenever a property is sold, an up-to-date copy of the folio and fileplan is obtained from the Land Registry and forms the backbone of the contract of sale. On the closing of a sale, searches are carried out to ensure that nothing else has been registered against the folio between the time that the copy was obtained and the closing, which may be weeks, if not months, later.

Registration of lands in the Land Registry is preferable to registration in the Registry of Deeds. Any land can be registered in the Land Registry provided the rules are followed and the necessary title documents are provided. The Land Registry is state guaranteed and if a Land Certificate is lost it can (eventually) be replaced, although at some cost. The title documents to a property which is not registered in the Land Registry cannot be replaced if lost, and only a copy of the memorial used to register the document in the Registry of Deeds can be obtained. This, however, can often be only a very short summary of the original document.

7:2.3 Time it takes to register lands

The time it takes to register land in the Land Registry varies depending on the county and according to the amount of work which may be involved in registration. If the property is part of a large housing estate, the Land Registry will first have to deal with the developer's registration and attend to the mapping of the development. A scheme map is lodged by the developer which shows the sites of each of the houses and the common areas servicing the development. Thereafter, the Land Registry will start to register each of the houses. However, in some cases this may take up to a year and after that it may take another six to nine months before the new houses will be registered. This should not concern any purchaser, as once the houses are purchased and the documents lodged then the purchaser is protected. However, copies of all documents should be kept in case the purchaser decides to sell the property before registration is completed.

The length of time it takes to register land will depend on how fast the documents needed for registration are processed by the solicitors and then by the various government agencies who are involved.

7:2.4 Title documents

7:2.4.1 Deeds of transfer and conveyance

The principal document which forms the basis of registering land is the deed of transfer or the deed of conveyance (*see* **Chapter 6, Completing a Purchase, para 6:4**). The term "deed of transfer" is used to refer to deeds which are lodged for registration in the Land Registry (*see* **para 6:5.2**). The term "deed of conveyance" is generally used to refer to deeds which are lodged for registration in the Registry of Deeds.

7:2.4.1.1 Deeds of conveyance

Deeds of conveyance pass the freehold title, that is, the entire legal ownerhsip, from one owner to another, while a deed of assignment passes a leasehold title from one person to another, the freehold being held by the head landlord. The term "deed of conveyance" can also be used to refer to a deed of transfer even where a leasehold title is being transferred. Both freehold and leasehold title can be registered in the Land Registry. The Land Certificate will state which register the lands are registered on, *i.e.* the register of freeholders or the register of leaseholders. Land Certificates may also be colour coded at the top right-hand corner of the front cover, with blue meaning freehold and red meaning leasehold. Freehold title differs from leasehold title in that freehold title never involves a landlord or the payment of rent.

7:2.4.1.2 Deeds of transfer

The deed of transfer contains several important paragraphs through which land is transferred from one person to another or to a series of other people. The first paragraph of the deed will state who the registered owner is, how much the property is being sold for and to whom, and how much money is being received by the owner from the purchaser (the receipt). The next part of the transfer consists of what lawyers call the "words of limitation", or how the property will be held by the purchasers, whether as joint tenants, tenants in common or subject to various terms, conditions and covenants and whether the property is held under a lease or in fee simple. The term "fee simple" or "in fee" means that the property is held without reference to any other superior interest in the property such as a landlord (*see* **Chapter 6, Completing a Purchase, para 6:4**).

The remainder of the deed consists of various certificates. The first one is called a section 45 certificate and refers to section 45 of the Land Act 1965 which provides that only qualified persons may purchase land outside of designated towns. Qualified persons are all Irish citizens and all E.U. nationals, as well as companies established in Ireland or the E.U. If a purchaser is not an Irish citizen or an E.U. national then the purchaser has to obtain the consent of the Minister for Agriculture.

The rest of the deed deals with revenue certificates which are required in order to have the deed properly stamped by the Revenue Commissioners. There are several kinds of revenue certificates but the main ones state what kind of property has been sold and whether the purchaser is a first time buyer, an owner-occupier or an investor. If the vendor and purchaser are related then the purchaser should ensure that the relevant certificate is included.

Finally, the deed is signed, sealed and delivered by both parties. The phrase "signed, sealed and delivered" signifies that the parties have signed and sealed the legal document and that the property has been delivered to the new owner. Traditionally, all legal documents selling property had to be sealed by the vendor and purchaser.

7:3 FLATS OR MAISONETTES

Since the 1970s, houses can only be sold in fee simple to purchasers, but flats and other properties can be sold under a lease. Lawyers like to use leases because rents can only be charged in leases and not where the freehold title of the property has been sold. Developers of blocks of flats or developments containing flats and commercial units will often try to derive an annual capital rent on their investment and will therefore try and charge an annual rent to the occupiers or tenants. However, it is uncommon for developers to charge a large amount for annual rent as most flat owners are not interested in paying an annual rent after having already expended a large amount of money purchasing the flat in the first place.

Blocks of flats require ongoing maintenance and those who develop or manage flats should establish a sinking fund to cover future capital expenditure. The "sinking fund" is a term generally used to refer to monies used to carry out major structural works, for instance, on the roof of a block of flats, or in replacing the central heating and air conditioning system. It may also refer to a more general fund from which all unplanned expenditure is paid, such as uninsured losses or accidents. The owners of flats will be required to pay an annual service charge to this sinking fund. Any prospective purchaser of either a new or a second-hand flat should enquire as to whether a sinking fund exists and how much is in the fund if it is already established.

Most blocks of flats and some housing estates will have a management company created in order to manage the common areas and ensure the efficient running of the block of flats and the common areas of the housing estate. The management company is composed of members who are the owners of the flats or houses as well as the original developer. The company pays the block insurance every year and also pays whatever outgoings are needed for maintenance including gardening, painting and normal wear and tear repairs. To fund these outgoings, all of the members of the company pay an annual fee or service charge to the management company based on the projected expenditure for the forthcoming year.

Most management companies will try to ensure that a separate capital fund is invested in from year to year, out of which larger projects can be accommodated. However, some management companies may not have such a fund and instead may expect the property owners to fund these projects when they are needed. There is an element of unfairness in this, especially if some of the property owners have not owned, or may not own, their properties for long and may be expected to contribute to something which they have not got, and will not get, any use.

7:3.1 Covenants, Conditions and Restrictive Clauses

Leases are used when selling flats because flats as properties have to rely on the flats below and above and on the common areas for physical support and access. Therefore, the lease will contain conditions restricting the use of the flat as well as covenants benefiting the flat.

Covenants are the terms of a lease which are of benefit to the owners of the flat, such as a provision that the owners of a flat are allowed free and unrestricted access to their property. The owners of houses may have covenants and conditions in their deeds of transfer or conveyance, especially in housing estates where there will be provisions for the use of the roads and services of the estate. There may also be covenants restricting the right of the owners of the houses. These restrictions could include a provision preventing the purchaser and successive owners using the house as a business or as a bed and breakfast. It is important for a purchaser to read through their purchase deeds and through the first deed, if purchasing the property from a previous owner, in order to see what kind of restrictions have been placed on the property. Some flats and houses may be situated on sites which share several pipes, wires or services with other houses on the estate. It is important for the owners to know where these are situated if problems arise, for instance if there is an electricity failure. Some property owners may find that their boundary fence or wall includes an electricity substation or sewer cover on which necessary maintenance may sometimes be carried out. Whenever maintenance work is carried out, the site or lands must, by law, be put back in the same condition as they were in before the works were carried out, although the payment of compensation to the property owner is usually excluded under the deed of transfer or conveyance.

Covenants can also be contained in deeds which transfer any type of land. A covenant is a binding agreement made between parties who intend the agreement to be binding indefinitely, with or without any money passing. There is a rule of law called the "rule against perpetuities" which prevents an open-ended provision being made for future events. For example, you cannot stipulate that an owner will be able to construct a roadway or lay pipes forever over a parcel of land. The rule prevents this type of stipulation, but does allow such a stipulation for future events for 21 years. This is why some deeds will state that all pipes, roads and service must be constructed now or within 21 years of the date of the deed.

Other covenants could include using neighbouring property to benefit the property being sold. For instance, there may be a covenant allowing adjoining property to be used as a percolation area or allowing water or sewer pipes to be placed on the property to connect them to the public services.

Purchasers (and vendors) must be aware of any conditions contained in the planning permission for the property which may be binding on all subsequent purchasers and which may act in the same way as a covenant. For instance, some planning permissions may stipulate that trees need to be replaced if they die within five years of construction. Therefore, the new owners of the property will need to also replace the trees in the place of the original owner.

It can be seen from the above that it is important that purchasers seek legal advice and assistance when dealing with problems relating to land and other land owners. This advice should be sought as soon as possible to avoid undue stress or incurring unnecessary financial outlays.

8 PROTECTION FROM BUILDING DEFECTS

8:1 INTRODUCTION

There are several avenues open to home-owners if problems arise with their house. Depending on the type of problem, the home-owner should first get a professional opinion; for instance, if the problem relates to shrinking, a structural engineer should be retained and a report obtained. Thereafter, purchasers should seek the advice of their solicitor. It is not necessary to consult the same solicitor used to purchase the property, but it is perfectly reasonable to do so, as he or she will have all of the relevant documents on file.

8:2 NEGLIGENCE AND BUILDERS

8:2.1 Caveat emptor ("let the buyer beware")

At common law a builder who built his own house on land and then sold it was generally able to avail of the principle of *caveat emptor* ("let the buyer beware"). However, this position has changed in recent years due to successive court decisions concerning the law relating to negligence and builders. This is mainly due to a distinct difference between the meaning of "defective premises" in the field of contract law and in tort. In tort (law relating to breaches of duty which give a right of action for damages), the "defects" commonly refer to dangerous defects which are a source of danger to the person or property of those who are likely to come onto the premises or find themselves in their vicinity.

8:2.2 Defects of quality

Defects of quality relate to defects in the condition of a premises which cause it to fall short of the standard of quality which was expected in a contract between a purchaser and a builder. These defects of quality are treated in a different way from defects caused by negligence. The remedy for defects of quality is by way of suing under the contract rather than suing for negligence. Therefore, it is important that a purchaser seeks the advice of a solicitor in order to establish the correct route to take in law against the builder once a defect has been spotted in the property.

8:2.3 Judicial law examined

There are a number of ways in which the courts have tried to assist property owners. The courts often recognise that where there is a contract between a builder and a purchaser, in the absence of express words to the contrary in the contract the builder is bound by three implied undertakings:

- that the builder would carry out the work in a good and workmanlike manner;
- that the builder will supply good and proper materials; and
- that the house will be built so as to ensure that it will be reasonably fit for human habitation if it is a dwelling.

English cases tended to hold that in the case of completed houses there was no implied warranty that the house be reasonably fit for habitation or that the builder had an obligation of care toward a future purchaser or future users of the property. However, this view has changed and the law in Ireland has developed from the principles set down in the case of *Donoghue v. Stevenson* ([1932] AC 562) which established the general principle that a man should be liable for foreseeable damage caused by his negligent acts. In the case of *Ward v. McMaster* ([1983] IR 29), the Irish courts held that a builder could be found liable for damages in negligence. The case concerned the construction of a house which was sub-standard, as well as structurally unsound and a source of risk, as well as a danger, to health. The house had been constructed by the owner on his site and the owner had lived in it for four years before selling it. The Court was satisfied, both in principle and based on previous case law, that the person who had built the property owed a duty of care to the person to whom he might subsequently sell it based on the neighbour principle established in *Donoghue v. Stevenson* and that on the facts of the case there was no reason to change this under contract or otherwise. The court held that the plaintiff could recover damages for both defects in quality and for inconvenience and dangerous defects.

Builders have in the past attempted to restrict liability through restrictive clauses in contracts. The courts have also rejected the use of a contract to exclude liability in negligence and confirmed that there was a right to sue under the contract as well as in a separate area of tort.

There have also been cases where a builder or developer made a statement which later turned out to be either false or misleading, as a result of which a purchaser suffered loss, inconvenience and expense.

An example of this was where purchasers relied on statements made by builders that their house would never have problems with damp. The purchasers bought the house based on that statement, even though the builder knew or ought to have known that the house would in fact have problems with damp later on.

In the case of *Hedley Byrne & Co. v. Heller & Partners Ltd* ([1964] AC 465), the House of Lords held that liability could arise from a negligent misstatement. The case arose from a negligent statement made by one bank regarding the creditworthiness of a customer which was then passed on to a company by the bank. On the particular facts of that case the court held that the bank was not liable, as the statement which was made by the bank contained a disclaimer of liability and was enough to prevent damages being awarded. However, the case did establish the principle in law that negligent misstatements can attract liability if a person relies on the defendant's special skill and trusts him or her to exercise due care.

8:2.4 Misstatements and misrepresentation

A further area or branch of the law which may be of relevance to house purchasers is the category of negligent misstatements or misrepresentation. The law may imply a duty of care where one person seeks information and trusts that the person giving the information has either a special skill, is a member of a profession or is in a special position to give that information and that a reliance is placed on that information being correct.

To continue with the example of a house which may be suffering from damp, if the builder or person selling the property believed that the property did not suffer from damp, but failed to carry out any examination of the property or have tests done on it, gave a statement to the purchaser confirming that there was no problem with damp, on which statement the purchaser acted, then the builder or seller may have given a negligent misstatement. However, the person giving the statement must be in a special position, such as being the builder of the property, rather than a simple homeowner. The misstatement or misrepresentation must have played a substantial part in inducing the plaintiff to act, and the person who has given the advice must have taken responsibility, in which case they will owe a duty of care to the person they are advising. There is nothing to prevent a builder from asserting that the advice or statement is being given without any responsibility as to its consequences, and this is often stated in the special conditions in the contract for sale of the property (*see* **Chapter 2, Deposits and Contracts, para 2:3**).

8:2.5 Recouping losses

Not all losses can be recouped even if a person is successful in an action for negligent misstatements or misrepresentations. Liability for economic loss due to negligent misrepresentations is based on the *Hedley Byrne* principle and is confined to cases where the statement or advice is given to a known recipient, *i.e.* an identifiable person, for a specific purpose and the recipient, to his or her detriment, relies and acts on the advice or statements given. An example of "economic loss" would be the cost of moving out of the house while the problem with damp was being remedied. The law draws a difference between the direct loss arising from a negligent action and consequential or economic losses which result from the negligent act and may or may not have been foreseeable.

8:2.6 Foundations and extras

It is common in a building agreement or contract for certain information about foundations or extras, such as the plans and specifications, to be given prior to the execution of the contract, and sometimes after the contract is signed. This information can be relied upon by both the purchaser and the builder or house owner and this reliance may result in an action for negligence if the information is misleading or wrong, apart from any possible action for fraud, which is a criminal offence.

8:3 SALE OF GOODS AND SUPPLY OF SERVICES ACT 1980

It should also be noted that Part V of the Sale of Goods and Supply of Services Act 1980 plays an important role in the law of misrepresentation in contracts. Section 44 removed the bars to recision of a contract for innocent misrepresentation imposed by the common law where the misrepresentation has become part of the contract or the contract has already been completed. Section 45(1) provides that if a person has entered into a contract after a misrepresentation and as a result suffers loss, then the person who has made the misrepresentation will be liable in damages, unless it is proven that the person who made the misrepresentation had reasonable grounds to believe, and did believe up to the time the contract was made, that the facts were true.

The Act also allows a court to award damages in lieu of ending a contract or not completing it provided that the innocent party is entitled to rescind the contract. Any provision in a contract purporting to exclude liability for misrepresentation is not enforceable unless it is shown to be fair and reasonable, with particular regard to be had to factors such as the strength of the bargaining position of the parties relative to each other and whether there was an inducement to agree to the term. For instance, a court could award damages against a builder who acted in such as way as to misrepresent a contract.

8:4 LIMITATION OF ACTIONS

There are a series of laws which restrict the right of a person to sue another in various areas of law and for different type of actions. Section 1(2) of the Statute of Limitations Act 1957 provides that an action which has its foundation in tort cannot be brought after six years from the date on which the action accrued; tort includes actions founded on negligence, such as negligent building. There are two exceptions to this provision, namely actions which claim damages for slander and actions which claim damages for negligence, nuisance or breach of duty where the damages consist of or include damages in respect of personal injury. A claim for personal injury has a three-year limitation period regardless of whether it arose out of a negligent act or a breach of contract.

The period of limitation begins to run from the date on which the cause of action accrued. That is when a complete and available cause of action first comes into existence. When the wrong is not actionable without showing actual damage, as in the case of negligence, then the cause of action cannot be said to be complete and the period of limitation cannot run until the damage occurs. In other words, the clock does not start until the damage occurs. In quite a few personal injuries cases the date on which the act was committed and the time at which the damage occurred would coincide, but there will be cases where they do not and the damage may only manifest itself years after the wrongful act was committed. Until a plaintiff is in a position to establish that damage has been caused, the cause of action is not complete and the period of limitation which is fixed by the Statute of Limitations does not commence.

Therefore, it is important to establish as soon as possible whether or not an action could exist and proceedings should be commenced well before the limitation period is due to expire. For instance, if serious cracks appear in a house, then after obtaining legal advice and possibly an engineer's report, the house owner should ensure that any proceedings are issued before the period of limitation may expire, either a period specified in the contract for the construction of the property, if there is one, or six years.

In some cases, for instance, where minor cracks appear in the plasterwork, the house owner will have to refer to the contract for the construction of the property. Frequently, the contract will stipulate the period in which a house owner will have to make a claim against the builder. Generally, the period allowed for minor defects under a contract for the construction of a house is six months, but in some cases this can be up to two years.

8:5 MAJOR AND MINOR DEFECTS

Contracts for the construction of houses will generally include some kind of reference to the builder's liability for major and minor structural defects. Usually, the purchaser of a house will receive a separate form of agreement from the builder. In some cases this agreement will be based on the HomeBond scheme (*see* **para 8:6**); in other cases it will be a separate agreement between the builder and the purchaser and can be assigned to subsequent purchasers. This agreement is generally referred to as a "structural defects indemnity".

8:5.1 Structural defects indemnity

The structural defects indemnity is basically a promise by a builder to remedy certain defects within an agreed period of time. The most common form of indemnity will allow a period of between six and 10 years during which a builder must remedy or defray the cost of remedying any major structural defect. Most indemnities will also allow for a period of six months during which the builder will remedy any minor defects. This ties in with the common building agreement, which also provides for a period of six months during which minor defects are remedied by the builder.

8:5.1.1 Limitation for major and minor defects

Frequently, the structural defects indemnity may not refer to remedying any minor defects, for which the purchaser will rely on the building agreement. Since the building agreement is a contract between the builder and the purchaser, there is a three-year limitation allowed for the enforcement of contracts under the Statute of Limitations. However, the building agreement limits that three-year period to a lesser one, usually six months. If the building agreement does not limit the period allowed to remedy minor defects, it can be argued that a purchaser would have the benefit of the three-year period of limitation in which he or she could expect the builder to remedy minor defects. In the case of major defects, these are limited to three years under the building agreement, unless the indemnity is obtained. Generally, major structural defects are not specifically defined. Instead, certain common defects or faults are listed as not being covered under the indemnity. The term "major structural defect" is usually taken to refer to any major defect in the foundation of the dwelling or the load bearing parts of the floors, walls, roof or the retaining walls. The definition is more or less the same as the definition used in the HomeBond scheme (*see* **para 8:6**).

8:5.1.2 What is not covered under the structural defects indemnity

The structural defects indemnity will not cover a defect which has been caused as a result of the negligent action of a third party, as a separate remedy will be available against third parties. Defects which are covered by a scheme of compensation provided for by legislation which is covered by insurance may also be excluded from the indemnity. However, this exclusion may not be accepted by some parties, and may also be contested by the insurance companies who provide cover. In any case the purchaser will only be concerned with getting the defect remedied and, in fact, need not be concerned with how the defects are remedied, as long as there is some level of protection obtained from the builder.

Other defects which may not be covered under a structural defects indemnity would be defects arising as a result of a mistake or negligent action on the part of the architect or engineer. This is why the architects and engineers used should have professional indemnity insurance. Hair cracks, shrinkage, expansion, dampness due to normal drying out of a dwelling house or condensation problems will be generally excluded under the indemnity. However, it should be remembered that a structural defects indemnity cannot exclude the builder from an action founded on negligence, except in very exceptional circumstances. The builder still has a duty of care toward the purchaser to ensure that the property is built in a good and workmanlike manner and that the materials used are fit for the purpose for which they were supplied. If the builder was in any way negligent about the way in which the property was built so that it suffered from shrinkage, then the structural defects indemnity cannot limit the builder's liability. General wear and tear or gradual deterioration is also usually excluded from the indemnity which the builder may provide.

8:5.1.3 Builders limiting their liability

Structural defects indemnities, while provided to offer extra cover for purchasers, will also try to limit the builder's own liability. Builders will try to limit the amount of compensation for which they may be liable either under the building agreement or under the structural defects indemnity. Liability for consequential loss will therefore be limited and, in most cases, totally excluded. "Consequential loss" includes such things as loss of wages incurred due to the purchaser trying to sort out a problem, or cleaning carpets after the builder has fixed the defect, unless the cleaning and replacement of carpets is so intrinsically linked to the defect that it is covered.

If the purchaser identifies any defects he or she must contact the builder in writing as soon as possible after the appearance of the defect.

8:5.1.4 Who carries out the repairs?

The structural defects indemnity will also provide that the builder, his servants and agents, have the right to enter the property at all reasonable times within normal working hours following reasonable notice to the purchaser so as to inspect the defect or to make good any defect. Sometimes this can be a particular bone of contention with the purchaser following the appearance of the defect, and some purchasers may insist on getting another builder to carry out the remedial works. However, most indemnities will not make such a provision and the builder can insist on carrying out the remedial works himself.

8:5.1.5 Liability for subsequent owners

Structural defects indemnities will generally also contain a clause which provides that the builder will not be liable, under the indemnity, to subsequent purchasers or owners of the property, if at the time of sale or at the time the property was acquired, the new owner knew or should have known of the defect or could have known of the defect after a reasonable examination by a competent surveyor, architect or engineer who would have disclosed the defect. The indemnity goes with the property to each of the successors in title until the time runs out, and is, therefore, an important title document.

8:6 THE HOMEBOND SCHEME

The HomeBond scheme guarantees a home against major structural defects for 10 years. The scheme is a service organised by the National House Building Guarantee Co. Ltd. and resulted from a joint venture between the Department of the Environment and the construction industry. The HomeBond company aims to set and maintain high standards of construction and provide financial indemnities in order to protect purchasers against loss of deposits or stage payments through the bankruptcy or liquidation of a builder. It also provides a 10-year warranty against structural faults.

The scheme guarantees the house against water and smoke penetration for the first two years and guarantees against the loss of a deposit or any stage payments before the house has been completed. The guarantees are only available from builders who are registered with the National House Building Guarantee Co. Ltd. Approximately 2,600 builders are members of HomeBond.

The stage payment protection repays lost deposits or contract payments which result from the registered builder's bankruptcy or liquidation subject to a maximum level of 15 per cent of the total purchase price of the house or €25,395, whichever is the lower. The protection operates from the date of registration for two years. The HomeBond scheme also provides for financial indemnity cover for the remainder of the contract, after the issue of HomeBond's final notice, which occurs after the main structural inspection carried out by a HomeBond inspector, of 50 per cent of the purchase price of the house or €63,487, again, whichever is the lower. This cover is designed with stage payments in mind and most lending institutions will insist on this type of cover where stage payments are involved.

This 50 per cent cover only lasts for six months after the issue of the final notice, which should be enough time to complete the construction of the house. The cover can be extended for six more months following a written request. These covers are separate from the two-year and 10-year warranties.

The HomeBond guarantee attaches to the property and passes on to each subsequent owner until the two- or 10-year periods expire, provided that the defects were not obvious at the time of the sale of the property.

8:6.1 How to claim under the HomeBond scheme

To act on a claim under the HomeBond scheme you must first write to the builder setting out the details of the defect and request that the necessary repairs be carried out. If the builder does not respond within 14 days, the purchaser must write to the HomeBond company and enclose a copy of the letter to the builder. The HomeBond company will then write to the builder and send out a technical expert to visit the site and carry out an inspection. Following the investigation, the builder must repair any defects within a reasonable time or else HomeBond will arrange for another builder to carry out the repairs at no expense to the purchaser.

If either the builder or the purchaser (home-owner) disputes the findings of the HomeBond inspector, then the matter may be remitted to an independent arbitrator who is appointed to adjudicate on the matter.

8:6.2 Major defects – houses

The definition of "major defect" in the case of a dwelling which is not an apartment (*see* **para 8:6.3**) is any major defect in the foundation of the dwelling or in the load-bearing parts of the floors, walls and roof or in any retaining walls necessary for the dwelling's support. In the HomeBond scheme the term "major defect" also covers any major defect to the dwelling, including apartments, which was caused directly by smoke damage arising from smoke penetration from the chimney breast into the habitable areas of the dwelling, but does not cover smoke penetration caused by down draught or by air starvation.

The scheme also covers any major defect caused by water penetration through the main structural elements, the roof flashings or the roof valleys of the dwelling.

8:6.3 Major defects – apartments

In the case of apartments, the term "major defect" covers any major defect in the foundation of the overall apartment building or in the load-bearing parts of its floors, walls and roof, or in any retaining walls which are necessary for the support of the building, which affects the structural stability of the building.

8:6.4 What is not covered under the HomeBond scheme

The HomeBond scheme does not cover damage which arises from hair cracks, shrinkage, expansion, dampness caused by normal drying out or condensation, wear and tear or gradual deterioration. The scheme also does not cover any defects in the central heating system. Defects arising from the installation or lifts and swimming pools are also excluded from the scheme, and purchasers should ensure that they receive an indemnity of some other form from the builder or the suppliers of these items.

8:7 COMPLETING ROADS, SERVICES AND COMMON AREAS

In most cases, the developer of a housing estate will complete the entire housing estate in good time and to a good standard of workmanship and skill. However, there may be occasions when the developer may not complete the entire estate, for instance, where not all of the houses are sold or not all of the houses have been built due to, for example, a slowdown in the economy.

In other cases, the roads or footpaths of an estate may need repair and general maintenance, but the developer will have finished the estate for some time and left the area for the next project. In these cases, the roads and services must be maintained by the builder, even though the builder has moved on. At the time the house was purchased, the solicitors acting for the purchaser received another indemnity from the builder. This indemnity covered the roads, footpaths, sewers, public lighting and water mains which serve the house and the rest of the housing development. This indemnity lasts until the local authority takes all of these services in charge.

Before the local authority will take over the maintenance of these services the authority will insist that the services and roads are in good condition and have been properly maintained. The local authority, as planning authority, may have already included a condition in the planning permission requiring the builder to complete the roads and services in the estate within a defined period. The local authority may have also insisted on a cash lodgement or the lodgement of a bond to cover the cost of the local authority completing, maintaining or repairing the roads and services. This bond or cash lodgement is usually released after the estate is properly completed or after the local authority takes the roads and services in charge.

If a problem arises with the roads and services in an estate, or serving a house, the purchaser must check that an indemnity exists and then pursue the builder to either complete or maintain the roads or services. If an indemnity does not exist, a purchaser still has the right to sue the builder under common law or under the building agreement in contract law. However, it is good conveyancing practice to demand a indemnity regarding the roads and services when purchasing a house from a developer.

Where a house is bought secondhand, the indemnity will go with the property to each of the subsequent purchasers until the roads and services are taken in charge by the local authority.

9 SELLING A HOUSE

9:1 INTRODUCTION

There are several things which a house owner should do before placing a house on the market. Most people tend to go first to the auctioneer and place the property on the market before going on to discuss the matter with anyone else. In fact, anyone interested in selling their house should first consult their solicitor. They may also need to consult a tax adviser or accountant to ascertain whether or not there are any tax implications in selling.

There are several simple questions a prospective seller should ask his or her solicitor, for example:

(a)   whether or not it is possible to sell the property; or

(b)   if not, how long it would take to get the proper legal title to allow the house to be sold. For instance, if the house has been recently purchased, the seller should make sure that his or her solicitor has the necessary paperwork completed. If, on the other hand, the property was purchased some time ago, or was recently inherited, there may be a great deal of legal work to be done.

A seller will have to decide how the property is to be sold. Most sellers will try to sell their property by way of private treaty, but some will sell through public auction. A sale by private treaty merely means that the seller and purchaser come to a private agreement, usually through an auctioneer, to agree on the price of the property and whether or not some of the contents are to be included.

9:2 LEGAL TITLE AND MORTGAGES

Even if the legal title to the property is in order and there are no tax problems, it may be the case that some work has been carried out on the house, for instance an extension or an alteration. In this case, an architect may have to carry out an inspection in order to make sure that the extension or alteration was carried out in compliance with planning permission and building regulations. Even if the works carried out on the house are classed as being exempt from requiring planning permission, a purchaser may insist that the seller provides a professional certificate of compliance with planning legislation and regulations (*see* **Chapter 3, Buying a Second-Hand House, para 3:2.6.1**).

It will be necessary for the seller to hand over the title documents to the purchasers of the property when the sale of the house is complete (*see* **Chapter 7, Registering Title**). However, it will also be necessary to forward copies of the title documents to the prospective purchaser as proof of title. Therefore, a prospective seller must make sure that copies of the title documents are available as soon as the house is sold.

In most cases the property will be registered in the Land Registry (*see* **Chapter 7, Registering Title, para 7:2.2**). It is advisable that sellers first obtain an up-to-date copy of the folio and a map (called a fileplan) from the Land Registry for €25. This will help during the course of selling the house, as it is useful to be able to refer to a map of the property. It is also advisable to obtain up-to-date copies of the registered title, as it may at an early stage indicate whether or not there is a problem with the title to the property, such as the use of an incorrect map.

As most properties will have a mortgage attached to them, the original title documents will be held by the mortgage lender until the mortgage is paid off. As the title documents are needed in order to complete the sale of the property, they will have to be obtained from the mortgage lender. This can only be done through a solicitor. This is because the solicitor will undertake, or promise, to hold the title documents in trust for the mortgage lender until the sale is complete, and thereafter to pay off the mortgage from the money received from the sale.

9:2.1 Mortgage balance

Anyone intending to sell a property with a mortgage should know how much is left owing to the mortgage lender. This is so that that they can be sure of how much will be left after the house is sold. The solicitor for the seller will also need to know how much there is left owing on the mortgage so that the solicitor can take this into account when dealing with the sale.

9:2.2 Legal costs

A seller should also make sure that he or she gets a written confirmation of the expected legal fees from his or her solicitor. Solicitors are obliged to forward, as soon as is practicable, written confirmation of the expected legal costs.

9:3 SALE BY PUBLIC AUCTION

Some people will decide to sell their property through a public auction. This is common where there is strong interest from potential buyers in the house being sold. It is generally the auctioneer who first suggests selling the property through a public auction. Selling any property by public auction can be stressful, as the auction can tend to focus emotions and will usually come after some weeks of potential buyers viewing the property. Some people will view houses out of curiosity rather than any real intention to purchase. Auctioneers may try to minimise the impact viewing has on owners by restricting viewing to one or two days when the owners are not present and the house has been "prepared". Getting a house ready for viewing can be a problem for all owners intending to sell their property, either by public auction or by private treaty. Personal items will have to be removed, the house will have to be cleaned and occupants may have to vacate the premises for the duration of the viewing period.

Where the property is sold by public auction it is usual to have the actual title documents on hand for inspection by bidders or their solicitors. In some countries, such as England, the sellers of properties are required to compile a file for prospective purchasers, including a structural survey (*see* **Chapter 3, Buying a Second-Hand House, para 3:2**). In Ireland, however, it is up to the purchasers to have a structural survey done. In the lead up to an auction, several structural surveys may be carried out on the house which is to be auctioned.

An auctioneer is the only person who is entitled to sell property by public auction in Ireland. No other person can sell property by public auction. An estate agent can sell houses on behalf of sellers and does not have to be an auctioneer, though most are. If an estate agent is not an auctioneer, he or she may not sell property by public auction.

At the beginning of the auction the auctioneer will stipulate the conditions of the contract for the sale of the house (*see* **Chapter 4, Deposits and Contracts, para 4:3.1 Special conditions**). The auctioneer may also indicate the expected closing date, *i.e.* when the purchase of the house is to be completed. Once the house has been sold by the auctioneer at auction, the contracts are signed by the successful bidder and a deposit is paid. In some cases the solicitor acting for the owner will read out the contract, and in most cases the solicitor for the owner will be present and will answer any queries regarding the title of the property.

9:4 AUCTIONEERS

Whichever way a house is sold, either by public auction or private treaty, most people will use an auctioneer or estate agent. It is advisable to engage the services of an auctioneer or bonded estate agent in order to offer some level of protection against negligence or fraudulent action on the part of the auctioneer or estate agent.

If an auctioneer or estate agent is used, the intended seller should find out exactly what fees will be charged.

As a seller, do not assume that the auctioneer's fees include advertising. Most auctioneers will charge separately for placing advertisements in local or national papers. In some cases the advertising of property costs a great deal of money. The intended seller should also make sure that the amount to be spent on advertising and the way in which the property is to be advertised is agreed in advance.

9:5 CONTENTS

Some properties will be sold with some of the household contents included, such as some kitchen items or some of the furniture (*see* **Chapter 3, Buying a Second-Hand House, para 3:3**). Some items must be included in the sale of a house, *i.e.* items which are regarded as being part of the essential fabric of the property. Examples of these would be the lights and light fittings, showers, shower doors or door handles. A good rule of thumb when deciding what is to be included in the sale of the house and what might be taken out prior to completing the sale is that if it takes a screwdriver or more to remove it, then it should probably stay.

If some of the contents are not included in the sale of the house, but the seller does not want to take them away, then it may be possible to include them in the sale of the house in consideration of an extra payment. If it is decided that some of the contents are included in the sale of the house, then a separate list is generally compiled for inclusion in the contract for the sale of the house.

In order to avoid any disagreements, auctioneers generally specify the contents to be included in the sale of the property in the sales advice note. The sales advice note is a letter stating the agreed price for the property, which it is not a contract for the sale of land in the legal sense.

9:6 TAX IMPLICATIONS, CAPITAL GAINS TAX, INHERITANCE TAX

The sale of any property in Ireland will attract some taxes. For example:

- If you use an auctioneer, VAT is charged on the auctioneer's fees.

- If the property is neither your home nor your principle private residence, the gain in the value of the property may be taxed as a capital gain.

- If the property has been inherited, some inheritance tax may be payable.

Note: The purchaser of the house may have to pay stamp duty, although the seller, generally, does not (*see* **Chapter 5, Stamp Duty**).

As tax legislation in Ireland is complex, sellers should obtain professional advice on the possible tax implications of selling their property. If the seller is selling their principle dwelling, there is probably no capital against tax payable on the gain in the value of the property between the date of purchase and the date of sale. However, this may not necessarily be the case. For instance, the house has to have been owned for more than 12 months and cannot be a holiday home, as a taxpayer can only have one principle dwelling for Capital Gains Tax purposes.

Therefore, as most sales will not be straightforward transactions where taxes are concerned, it is crucial that sellers obtain proper tax advice.

9:7 FAMILY LAW

Unfortunately, sometimes sellers will have experienced marital difficulties which will have implications with regard to selling a house, especially a family home. In law, the definition of a family home is a place where a married couple ordinarily reside. This definition can also include a holiday home and even a houseboat. The seller will have to inform his or her solicitor about the situation and it may be necessary to draft a family home declaration (*see* **Chapter 6, Completing a Purchase, Para 6:3.1**) which includes the particular situation.

Even where there are no marital difficulties, if the seller is married but is the only, or sole owner of a house, his or her spouse must consent to the sale of the house before it can be sold. The Family Home Protection Act 1976 provides that the sale of any family home which is not consented to by the spouse of an owner before the sale is null and void. It is therefore important that a spouse sign a consent before the contracts are signed by the other spouse.

9:8 CLOSING A SALE

Closing the sale of a house is not a very complicated procedure for a seller as most of the work will already have been done by the time the sale comes to be completed. The solicitor for the seller will have completed the necessary closing documents and will have asked the seller to come in and sign them in advance of receiving the purchase money from the solicitor for the purchaser (*see* **Chapter 6, Completing a Purchase, para 6:3**).

The solicitor will have prepared a deed of transfer or conveyance which passes the legal title from the seller to the buyer (*see* **Chapter 7: Registering Title, para 7:2.4.1**). The solicitor will also have prepared a family home declaration which covers the various pieces of legislation relating to family law, together with whatever closing documents are necessary.

Before the sale of a house is completed, the solicitor for the seller will often ask that up-to-date receipts are available. This is so that the seller can show to the purchaser that all bills have been paid. These bills would include the ESB, telephone, cable television and refuse charges.

The seller will also have cleared out the house and handed over all the keys to the property either to the solicitor dealing with the sale or to the auctioneer.

GLOSSARY

Certificate of Compliance	refers to a certificate usually given by an architect confirming that a property is built in compliance with planning law
Charge	a term used to refer to a mortgage or loan registered against property
Closing	a term used to refer to the completion of a sale or purchase where money is handed over in return for possessions
Convey	the legal term used to refer to the legal transfer of ownership
Covenants	a legal term used to refer to a restrictive condition
Deed of Conveyance/ Deed of Transfer	a legal document transferring legal title in land from one person to another
Deed of Assignment	a legal document which transfers the interest in a leased property from one person to another
Discharge (or Vacate)	a legal term used to refer to a document confirming that a loan has been paid
Drawing down	receiving the loan cheque or mortgage cheque
Early redemption penalty	an extra charge put on a mortgage if the mortgage is paid off early (only applied on fixed rate mortgages)
Folio	the file or record of ownership of land registered in the Land Registry
Land Certificate	a legal title document showing the ownership of property registered in the Land Registry
Land Registry	the State body charged with overseeing the registration of lands

Letter of loan offer	the contract between a borrower and the mortgage company giving details of the loan and the attaching conditions
Mortgage	a charge or an interest in property given as a result of lending money to a landowner
Mortgagee	the person giving a mortgage, *i.e.* a bank or building society
Mortgagor	the person taking out a mortgage
Percolation area	an area of ground adjacent to a septic tank which absorbs run-off water.
Professional indemnity insurance	an insurance policy taken out by professionals, such as solicitors, engineers, and architects, protecting third parties, usually clients, against any damage caused as a result of a negligent act committed by the professional
Registry of Deeds	a central registry situated in Henrietta Street, Dublin for the registration of legal documents, principally relating to land
Root of title	a legal reference to the principle legal title document, usually between 20 and 40 years old
Section 72 declaration	one of the closing documents signed by the vendor and referring to the provisions of section 72 of the Land Act 1965
Sinking fund	a fund held, usually by an investment company, to provide for repairs or the rebuilding of a block of flats
Undertaking	an agreement given by a solicitor to carry out legal work, usually on behalf of a bank, such as to hand over title documents

APPENDIX 1 — USEFUL ADDRESSES

Department of the Environment and Local Government
Head Office
Custom House
Dublin 1
Tel: (01) 888 2000
LoCall: (1890) 20 20 21

Department of the Environment and Local Government
Government Buildings
New House Grant
Ballina
Co. Mayo
Tel: (096) 242 00
    (01) 888 2002
LoCall: (1890) 30 50 30

HomeBond Co. Ltd.
Land Registry
Central Office
Chancery St.
Dublin 7
Tel: (01) 670 7500
LoCall: (1890) 333 001
(for the counties of Cavan, Louth, Monaghan, Donegal, Leitrim, Longford, Meath and Westmeath)

Land Registry
Block 1
Irish Life Centre
Lower Abbey St.
Dublin 1
Tel: (01) 670 7500
LoCall: (1890) 333 001
(for the counties of Kildare and Wicklow)

Land Registry
Setanta Centre
Nassau St.
Dublin 2
Tel: (01) 670 7500
LoCall: (1890) 333 001
(for the counties of Dublin and all counties west of the Shannon)

Land Registry
New Government Buildings
Cork Road
Waterford
Tel: (051) 303 000
LoCall: (1890) 333 002
(for the counties of Cork, Kerry, Limerick, Waterford, Carlow, Kilkenny, Wexford, Laois, Offaly, and Tipperary)

Law Society of Ireland
Blackhall Place
Dublin 7
Tel: (01) 672 4800

Ordnance Survey
Phoenix Park
Dublin 8
Tel: (01) 802 5300

Registry of Deeds
Henrietta St.
Dublin 1
Tel: (01) 670 7500
LoCall: (1890) 333 001

Revenue Commissioners
Dublin Castle
Dublin 2
Tel: (01) 647 5000
(for Capital Acquisitions Tax, Residential Property Tax and Stamp Duty)

The addresses of the various local authorities are available in each of the local telephone directories.

INDEX

References are to paragraph numbers.